Dirt Bikes

By Danny Parr

Consultant:
Hugh Fleming
Director, AMA Sports
American Motorcyclist Association

CAPSTONE
HIGH-INTEREST
BOOKS

an imprint of Capstone Press
Mankato, Minnesota

Capstone High-Interest Books are published by Capstone Press
151 Good Counsel Drive, P.O. Box 669, Mankato, Minnesota 56002
http://www.capstone-press.com

Library of Congress Cataloging-in-Publication Data
Parr, Danny.
    Dirt bikes/by Danny Parr.
    p. cm.—(Wild rides)
    Includes bibliographical references and index.
    ISBN 0-7368-0927-9
    1. Trail bikes—Juvenile literature. [1. Trail bikes. 2. Motorcycling.] I. Title.
II. Series.
TL441 .P37 2002
629.227'5—dc21   2001000210

Summary: Discusses these small motorcycles, their history, parts, and
competitions.

Editorial Credits
Matt Doeden, editor; Karen Risch, product planning editor; Kia Bielke,
    cover and interior designer; Katy Kudela, photo researcher

Photo Credits
ALLSPORT PHOTOGRAPHY, 26
FPG International LLC, 8, 10–11
Isaac Hernandez/Mercury Press, 17
Jim Sanderson, 12, 18, 22, 28
Larry Prosor, cover, 14
Mark Kariya, 24
Richard Cummins/Photophile, 4, 7, 20–21

1 2 3 4 5 6 07 06 05 04 03 02

Table of Contents

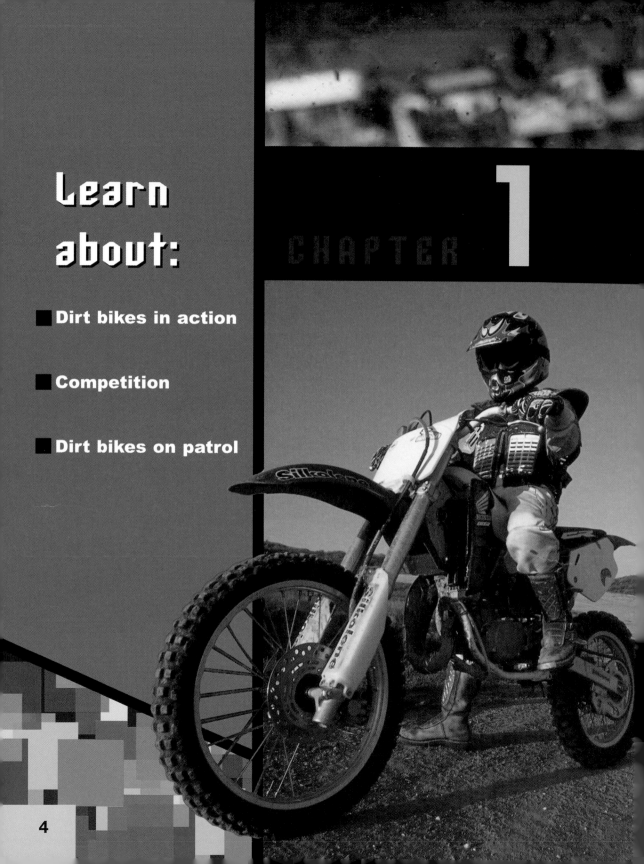

Learn about:

- **Dirt bikes in action**

- **Competition**

- **Dirt bikes on patrol**

CHAPTER 1

Dirt Bikes

A bright yellow dirt bike speeds over a large mound of dirt. The rider pulls up slightly on the handlebars as the bike reaches the top of the mound. The bike and the rider sail through the air.

The rider holds on tightly as the dirt bike lands. The crowd cheers loudly for the jump. But the rider does not stop. Seven other riders follow close behind.

The rider speeds to the next turn. He puts his foot down as he enters a sharp turn. He then accelerates toward the final jump. But he hears the other riders behind him. He knows he must jump perfectly to win the race.

About Dirt Bikes

Dirt bikes are motorcycles built to ride on dirt tracks and off-road courses. Dirt bikes handle well on dirt, mud, sand, and grass. Riders enjoy riding dirt bikes away from roads and highways.

Most dirt bikes are built higher off the ground than street motorcycles. They need extra clearance on bumpy trails. Clearance is the space between the ground and the bottom of a motorcycle.

Dirt bikes are lighter than street motorcycles. Their light weight makes them fast and quick. Dirt bikes can make sharp turns that street motorcycles cannot make.

Dirt Bike Uses

Many dirt bikes are used in competitions. Dirt bikes such as motocross cycles are built for racing on dirt tracks. Some dirt bikes are built for long off-road races called enduros. Others are built for performing aerial stunts. Riders perform these tricks in the air.

People use dirt bikes for more than competitions. Some members of the Royal

Canadian Mounted Police patrol on dirt bikes. Forest rangers sometimes ride dirt bikes instead of horses. Some cowboys even use dirt bikes to herd cattle.

Most people ride dirt bikes for fun. They can explore areas on dirt bikes that cars and street motorcycles cannot explore.

Riders can explore areas on dirt bikes that cars and street motorcycles cannot explore.

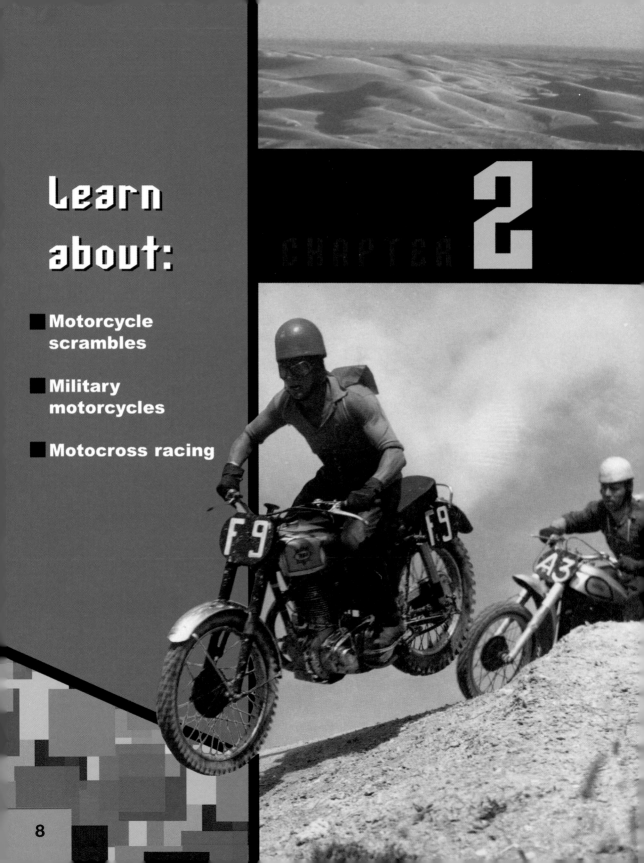

Learn about:

- Motorcycle scrambles

- Military motorcycles

- Motocross racing

CHAPTER **2**

Early Models of Dirt Bikes

Motorcycles were invented in the late 1800s. In 1885, a German man named Gottlieb Daimler built a motorcycle. People called Daimler's motorcycle a boneshaker because it gave the rider a very rough ride.

People soon began racing motorcycles. Early motorcycle riders raced against cars. But these races were dangerous. Cars did not handle as well as motorcycles. Cars could accidentally hit or run over the motorcycles. By the 1900s, people began holding races just for motorcycles.

Cross-Country Cycles

Early motorcycles worked well only on smooth surfaces. Riders could not ride the motorcycles on rough tracks or off roads.

In 1899, an American man named E.J. Pennington built a new, more durable type of motorcycle. He advertised his motorcycle as a cross-country motorcycle. His advertisement showed a picture of a rider jumping over a river. Pennington's motorcycle could not really

perform that type of stunt. But it could handle rougher treatment than earlier models. Pennington's motorcycle helped change the way people thought about motorcycles.

In 1924, the first motorcycle scramble took place in England. This event was the first major off-road, cross-country motorcycle race. Scrambles quickly became popular in England and France. Some French riders began calling scrambles "motocross."

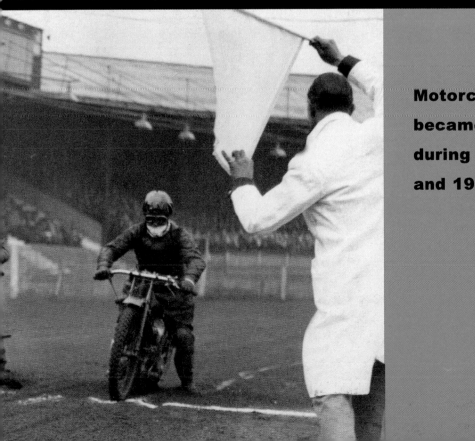

Motorcycle racing became popular during the 1930s and 1940s.

Motorcycles at War

Two major wars took place in Europe during the early 1900s. Military forces used cross-country motorcycles during World War I (1914–1918) and World War II (1939–1945).

Motorcycle riders carried messages to and from the trenches. Most of the fighting took

Motocross racing quickly became one of the most popular types of dirt bike racing.

place in these areas. This work was dangerous. Riders had little protection from enemy fire. They often had to ride over rough, muddy ground. The motorcycles sometimes became stuck in the mud. Riders who became stuck were easy targets for enemy fire.

Dirt Bikes

Modern racing dirt bikes were designed in the 1950s. Manufacturers built lightweight, sturdy bikes for off-road racing. They removed unnecessary parts such as the lights and fenders. They added suspension systems to make the ride less bumpy. People began calling these motorcycles "dirt bikes."

Motocross racing began in the United States in the 1960s. Riders raced on dirt tracks. The tracks included jumps and sharp turns.

Motocross soon became a popular sport across North America. People wanted to buy their own dirt bikes. Most people bought bikes built by Japanese manufacturers. A company called Honda built the most popular dirt bikes.

Learn about:

CHAPTER 3

- **Shock absorbers**

- **Internal combustion engines**

- **Customization**

Designing a Dirt Bike

Many types of dirt bikes exist today. Each type is built differently. But all dirt bikes have the same basic parts. Riders often modify these parts to suit their needs. These small changes improve the dirt bikes' performance.

Tires and Suspension

Most dirt bikes have small, flexible tires. Most of these tires have deep tread. This pattern of bumps and deep grooves on a tire gives a dirt bike good traction. Traction allows the wheels to grip surfaces covered with loose dirt and mud.

Suspension systems connect the wheels to the bike's main body. These systems include shock absorbers that help riders ride smoothly over bumpy ground.

Engines

Dirt bikes have either two-stroke or four-stroke engines. Two-stroke engines allow riders to quickly accelerate to high speeds. Motocross cycles use these engines. Four-stroke engines do not accelerate as quickly. But they are more powerful and use less fuel. Some enduro bikes use four-stroke engines.

All dirt bike engines are internal combustion engines. These engines combine fuel and air inside a tube-shaped part called a cylinder. A spark plug inside the cylinder causes the fuel to explode. These explosions cause a piston inside the cylinder to move up and down. The piston's movement provides the engine's power.

Controls

Riders use a variety of controls to ride their dirt bikes. Three of the most important controls are on the handlebars. They are the throttle, the brake, and the clutch. The rider controls the throttle and the brake with the right hand. The throttle is a twist-grip. The rider twists the grip to speed up. Riders use the brake to slow down.

The rider controls the clutch with the left hand. Riders must pull the clutch to shift gears. The gear lever usually is under the left foot. On most dirt bikes, the rider presses down on the lever for first gear. The rider pulls the lever up one spot for each higher gear. This gear arrangement is called "one down, four up."

Dirt bikes have small internal combustion engines.

Dirt bike riders customize their bikes to fit their riding styles.

Customizing Dirt Bikes

Dirt bike riders want bikes that fit their riding styles. They modify their bikes to meet their needs. This process is called customizing.

Most riders do some basic customizing. For example, they adjust the height and angle of the seat. Riders also may add seat covers. These covers add extra seat padding. Some seat covers help prevent the rider from slipping off the seat during sharp turns.

Riders also adjust the angle of the handlebars. Riders may shorten or lengthen the handlebars. Short handlebars allow for easier small turns. Long handlebars make sharp turns easier.

Riders can customize many other features on their bikes. They may adjust the position of the brake levers or gear levers. They may add detailing to their dirt bikes. Detailing includes painted artwork and stickers glued on the bike.

Parts of a Dirt Bike

Rear Fender

Exhaust

Engine

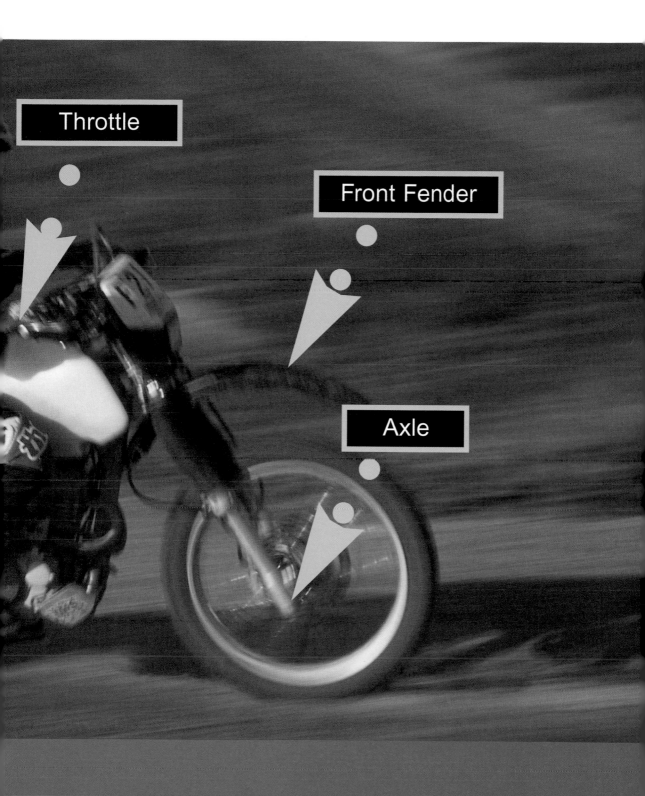

Throttle

Front Fender

Axle

Learn about:

- **Track features**

- **Series championships**

- **Paris-Dakar race**

CHAPTER 4

Dirt Bikes in Competition

Dirt bike riders may take part in different types of races. Short track races are popular for riders of all skill levels. Some racers take part in long, off-road events. Others race across dangerous areas such as deserts. Riders use different types of dirt bikes in each type of competition.

Motocross and Supercross

Motocross is the most popular type of dirt bike racing. Motocross racers race on short outdoor tracks. Supercross racing is similar to motocross. But supercross racers compete on indoor tracks.

Motocross and supercross tracks include bumps and jumps. A sloped pile of dirt on a corner is called a berm. A berm's slope helps riders turn sharp corners without slowing down.

Professional motocross riders may race in a series. Riders score points for many different races during a series. The rider with the best score after all of the races wins the series championship. The most popular series is the World Championship Motocross Series.

Enduro racers compete on long dirt courses.

Motocross cycles are small and powerful. Their two-stroke engines allow them to accelerate quickly. Motocross cycle engines are classified by size. Engine size is measured in cubic centimeters (cc). Small cycles may have engines as small as 50cc. Professional riders usually ride 125cc or 250cc cycles.

Enduros

Enduro racers compete on long dirt courses. Many enduro courses are about 150 miles (241 kilometers) long. Some are longer.

Enduro racers must ride at a set speed. Race officials give penalty points to riders who go too slow or too fast. The rider with the fewest penalty points at the end of the race wins.

Enduro bikes are sturdy. Their four-stroke engines allow riders to travel long distances without stopping for fuel.

Enduro bikes also have equipment that most dirt bikes do not have. They have headlights, taillights, and a speedometer. The speedometer helps racers keep track of their speed and the distance they have traveled.

Desert racers cross large deserts to win races.

Desert Racing

Desert races may be more than 1,000 miles (1,600 kilometers) long. They may take a day or longer to complete. Riders work in teams of two to complete a desert race.

Desert racers must cross a desert to reach the finish line. One famous desert race is the Paris-Dakar race. Riders in this race travel from Paris, France, to Dakar, Senegal. Riders must travel about 7,000 miles (11,270 kilometers) across the Sahara Desert in Africa. The race takes about 18 days to complete.

Another popular desert race is the Baja race. Riders in this race must cross a desert in northern Mexico. This race is about 1,000 miles (1,600 kilometers) long.

Desert racing bikes must be comfortable and dependable. They have large, cushioned seats. Riders carry food and water on their bikes. Desert racing bikes have four-stroke engines with large gas tanks.

Ricky Carmichael

Ricky Carmichael was born November 27, 1979, in Clearwater, Florida. He began racing motorcycles at age 5. He raced as an amateur for 11 years. He won 67 amateur championships during this time.

Carmichael began racing as a professional in 1996. He won the AMA 125cc National Motocross Championship in his first year of racing. He won the title again the following year.

Today, Carmichael races in both motocross and supercross events. He is one of the most successful and popular racers in the sport. He even has a video game named after him.

Words to Know

accelerate (ak-SEL-uh-rate)—to gain speed

berm (BURM)—a banked turn or corner on a motocross track

clearance (KLIHR-uhnss)—the distance between the ground and the bottom of a motorcycle

clutch (KLUHCH)—a lever that a motocross rider must pull in order to shift gears

cylinder (SIL-uhn-dur)—a hollow chamber inside an engine where fuel is burned

modify (MOD-uh-fye)—to change a motorcycle in order to improve performance

piston (PIS-tuhn)—a part inside an engine cylinder that moves back and forth as fuel is burned

throttle (THROT-uhl)—a grip or lever that controls how much fuel and air flow into an engine; a dirt bike rider twists the throttle to speed up.

tread (TRED)—a series of bumps and deep grooves on a tire; tread helps tires grip surfaces.

To Learn More

Pupeza, Lori Kinstad. *Dirt Bikes.* Ultimate Motorcycle. Minneapolis: Abdo & Daughters, 1999.

Schaefer, Adam. *Motocross Cycles.* Wild Rides! Mankato, Minn.: Capstone High-Interest Books, 2002.

Young, Jesse. *Dirt Bikes.* Motorcycles. Mankato, Minn.: Capstone Books, 1995.

Useful Addresses

American Motorcyclist Association
13515 Yarmouth Drive
Pickerington, OH 43147

Canadian Motorcycle Association
P.O. Box 448
Hamilton, ON L8L 1J4
Canada

Internet Sites

American Motorcyclist Association

http://www.amadirectlink.com/index.asp

The Canadian Motorcycle Association

http://www.canmocycle.ca

MotoWorld.com

http://www.motoworld.com

Index